Seven Dada Manifestos

and

Lampisteries

TRISTAN TZARA
Seven Dada Manifestos
and
Lampisteries

Translated by
Barbara Wright

Illustrations by Francis Picabia

CALDER PUBLICATIONS · RIVERRUN PRESS
London Paris New York

This edition published in Great Britain in 1992 by
Calder Publications Limited
9-15 Neal Street, London WC2H 9TU

and in the United States of America in 1992 by
Riverrun Press Inc.
1170 Broadway, New York, NY 10001

First published in Great Britain in 1977 by
John Calder (Publishers) Ltd and in the United States of America in 1981 by
Riverrun Press Inc.

Third impression 1984
Fourth impression 1992

First published in this edition in France in 1963 by
Editions Jean-Jacques Pauvert as *Sept manifestes Dada, lampisteries*

ISBN 0 7145 3762 4

Cataloguing in Publication Data is available from the British Library
Cataloging in Publication Data is available from the Library of Congress

Photoset in Great Britain by Specialist Offset Services Ltd., Liverpool.
Printed and bound in the United States of America by the Maple-Vail Book Manufacturing Group, Pennsylvania.

CONTENTS

Seven Dada Manifestos

MONSIEUR ANTIPYRINE'S MANIFESTO

DADA is our intensity: it erects inconsequential bayonets and the Sumatral head of German babies; Dada is life with neither bedroom slippers nor parallels; it is against and for unity and definitely against the future; we are wise enough to know that our brains are going to become flabby cushions, that our antidogmatism is as exclusive as a civil servant, and that we cry liberty but are not free; a severe necessity with neither discipline nor morals and that we spit on humanity.

DADA remains within the framework of European weaknesses, it's still shit, but from now on we want to shit in different colours so as to adorn the zoo of art with all the flags of all the consulates.

We are circus ringmasters and we can be found whistling amongst the winds of fairgrounds, in convents, prostitutions, theatres, realities, feelings, restaurants, ohoho, bang bang.

We declare that the motor car is a feeling that has cosseted us quite enough in the dilatoriness of its abstractions, as have transatlantic liners, noises and ideas. And while we put on a show of being facile, we are actually searching for the central essence of things, and are pleased if we can hide it; we have no wish to count the windows of the marvellous élite, for DADA doesn't exist for anyone, and we want everyone to understand this. This is Dada's balcony, I assure you. From there you can hear all the military marches, and come down cleaving the air like a seraph landing in a public baths to piss and understand the parable.

DADA is neither madness, nor wisdom, nor irony, look at me, dear bourgeois.

Art used to be a game of nuts in May, children would go gathering words that had a final ring, then they would exude, shout out the verse, and dress it up in dolls' bootees, and the verse became a queen in order to die a little, and the queen became a sardine, and the children ran hither and yon, unseen ... Then came the great ambassadors of feeling, who yelled historically in chorus:

Psychology Psychology hee hee

Science Science Science

Long live France

We are not naive

We are successive

We are exclusive

We are not simpletons

and we are perfectly capable of an intelligent discussion.

But we, DADA, don't agree with them, for art isn't serious, I assure you, and if we reveal the crime so as to show that we are learned denunciators, it's to please you, dear audience, I assure you, and I adore you.

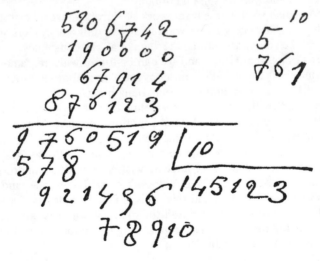

II
DADA MANIFESTO
1918

*The magic of a word — DADA —
which for journalists has opened
the door to an unforeseen world,
has for us not the slightest
importance.*

To launch a manifesto you have to want: A.B. & C., and fulminate
against 1, 2, & 3,
work yourself up and sharpen your wings to conquer and circulate
lower and upper case As, Bs & Cs, sign, shout, swear, organise
prose into a form that is absolutely and irrefutably obvious, prove
its ne plus ultra and maintain that novelty resembles life in the same
way as the latest apparition of a harlot proves the essence of God.
His existence had already been proved by the accordion, the
landscape and soft words. ☆ To impose one's A.B.C. is only
natural — and therefore regrettable. Everyone does it in the form
of a crystalbluff-madonna, or a monetary system, or
pharmaceutical preparations, a naked leg being the invitation to an
ardent and sterile Spring. The love of novelty is a pleasant sort of
cross, it's evidence of a naive don't-give-a-damn attitude, a passing,
positive, sign without rhyme or reason. But this need is out of date,
too. By giving art the impetus of supreme simplicity — novelty —
we are being human and true in relation to innocent pleasures;
impulsive and vibrant in order to crucify boredom. At the lighted
crossroads, alert, attentive, lying in wait for years, in the forest. ☆
I am writing a manifesto and there's nothing I want, and yet I'm
saying certain things, and in principle I am against manifestos, as I
am against principles (quantifying measures of the moral value of
every phrase — too easy; approximation was invented by the

3

impressionists). ☆

I'm writing this manifesto to show that you can perform contrary actions at the same time, in one single, fresh breath; I am against action; as for continual contradiction, and affirmation too, I am neither for nor against them, and I won't explain myself because I hate common sense.

DADA — this is a word that throws up ideas so that they can be shot down; every bourgeois is a little playwright, who invents different subjects and who, instead of situating suitable characters on the level of his own intelligence, like chrysalises on chairs, tries to find causes or objects (according to whichever psychoanalytic method he practises) to give weight to his plot, a talking and self-defining story. ☆

Every spectator is a plotter, if he tries to explain a word (to know!) From his padded refuge of serpentine complications, he allows his instincts to be manipulated. Whence the sorrows of conjugal life.

To be plain: The amusement of redbellies in the mills of empty skulls.

   DADA DOES NOT MEAN ANYTHING

If we consider it futile, and if we don't waste our time over a word that doesn't mean anything ... The first thought that comes to these minds is of a bacteriological order: at least to discover its etymological, historical or psychological meaning. We read in the papers that the negroes of the Kroo race call the tail of a sacred cow: DADA. A cube, and a mother, in a certain region of Italy, are called: DADA. The word for a hobby-horse, a children's nurse, a double affirmative in Russian and Roumanian, is also: DADA. Some learned journalists see it as an art for babies, other Jesuscallingthelittlechildrenuntohim saints see it as a return to an unemotional and noisy primitivism — noisy and monotonous. A sensitivity cannot be built on the basis of a word; every sort of construction converges into a boring sort of perfection, a stagnant idea of a golden swamp, a relative human product. A work of art shouldn't be beauty *per se*, because it is dead; neither gay nor sad, neither light nor dark; it is to rejoice or maltreat individualities to serve them up the cakes of sainted haloes or the sweat of a meandering chase through the atmosphere. A work of art is never beautiful, by decree, objectively, for everyone. Criticism is, therefore, useless; it only exists subjectively, for every individual, and without the slightest general characteristic. Do people imagine they have found the psychic basis common to all humanity? The attempt of Jesus, and the Bible, conceal, under their ample, benevolent wings: shit, animals and days. How can anyone hope to order the chaos that constitutes that infinite, formless variation: man? The principle: "Love thy neighbour" is hypocrisy. "Know thyself" is utopian, but more acceptable because it includes malice. No pity. After the carnage we are left with the hope of a purified humanity. I always speak about myself because I don't want to convince, and I have no right to drag others in my wake, I'm not compelling anyone to follow me, because everyone makes his art in his own way, if he knows anything about the joy that rises like an arrow up to the astral strata, or that which descends into the mines strewn with the flowers of corpses and fertile spasms. Stalactites: look everywhere for them, in creches magnified by pain, eyes as white as angels' hares. Thus DADA was born*, out of a need for independence, out of mistrust for the community. People who join us keep their freedom. We don't accept any theories. We've had enough of the cubist and futurist academies: laboratories of formal ideas. Do we make art in order to earn money and keep the dear bourgeoisie happy? Rhymes have the smack of money, and inflexion slides along the line of the stomach in profile. Every group of artists has ended up at this bank, straddling various comets. Leaving the door open to the possibility of wallowing in comfort and food.

Here we are dropping our anchor in fertile ground.

Here we really know what we are talking about, because we have experienced the trembling and the awakening. Drunk with energy, we are revenants thrusting the trident into heedless flesh. We are streams of curses in the tropical abundance of vertiginous

* In 1916 at the CABARET VOLTAIRE in Zurich.

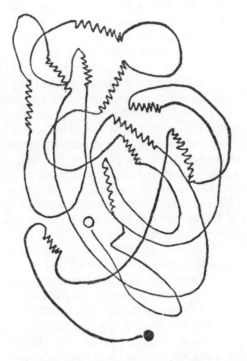

vegetation, resin and rain is our sweat, we bleed and burn with thirst, our blood is strength.

Cubism was born out of a simple manner of looking at objects: Cézanne painted a cup twenty centimetres lower than his eyes, the cubists look at it from above, others complicate its appearance by cutting a vertical section through it and soberly placing it to one side. (I'm not forgetting the creators, nor the seminal reasons of unformed matter that they rendered definitive.) ☆ The futurist sees the same cup in movement, a succession of objects side by side, mischievously embellished by a few guide-lines. This doesn't stop the canvas being either a good or a bad painting destined to form an investment for intellectual capital. The new painter creates a world whose elements are also its means, a sober, definitive, irrefutable work. The new artist protests: he no longer paints (symbolic and illusionistic reproduction) but creates directly in stone, wood, iron, tin, rocks, or locomotive structures capable of being spun in all directions by the limpid wind of the momentary sensation. ☆ Every pictorial or plastic work is unnecessary, even if it is a monster which terrifies servile minds, and not a sickly-sweet object to adorn the refectories of animals in human garb, those illustrations of the sad fable of humanity. — A painting is the art of making two lines, which have been geometrically observed to be parallel, meet on a canvas, before our eyes, in the reality of a world that has been transposed according to new conditions and possibilities. This world is neither specified nor defined in the work, it belongs, in its innumerable variations, to the spectator. For its creator it has neither cause nor theory. *Order = disorder; ego = non-ego; affirmation = negation*: the supreme radiations of an absolute art. Absolute in the purity of its cosmic and regulated chaos, eternal in that globule that is a second which has no duration, no breath, no light and no control. ☆ I appreciate an old work for its novelty. It is only contrast that links us to the past. ☆ Writers who like to moralise and discuss or ameliorate psychological bases have, apart from a secret wish to win, a ridiculous knowledge of life, which they have classified, parcelled out, canalised; they are determined to see its categories dance when they beat time. Their readers laugh derisively, but carry on: what's the use?

There is one kind of literature which never reaches the voracious masses. The work of creative writers, written out of the author's real necessity, and for his own benefit. The awareness of a supreme egoism, wherein laws become insignificant. ☆ Every page should explode, either because of its profound gravity, or its vortex, vertigo, newness, eternity, or because of its staggering absurdity, the enthusiasm of its principles, or its typography. On the one hand there is a world tottering in its flight, linked to the resounding tinkle of the infernal gamut; on the other hand, there are: the new men. Uncouth, galloping, riding astride on hiccups. And there is a mutilated world and literary medicasters in desperate need of amelioration.

I assure you: there is no beginning, and we are not afraid; we aren't sentimental. We are like a raging wind that rips up the clothes of clouds and prayers, we are preparing the great spectacle of disaster, conflagration and decomposition. Preparing to put an end to mourning, and to replace tears by sirens spreading from one continent to another. Clarions of intense joy, bereft of that poisonous sadness. ☆ DADA is the mark of abstraction; publicity and business are also poetic elements.

I destroy the drawers of the brain, and those of social organisation: to sow demoralisation everywhere, and throw heaven's hand into hell, hell's eyes into heaven, to reinstate the fertile wheel of a universal circus in the Powers of reality, and the fantasy of every individual.

A philosophical question: from which angle to start looking at life, god, ideas, or anything else. Everything we look at is false. I don't think the relative result is any more important than the choice of pâtisserie or cherries for dessert. The way people have of looking hurriedly at things from the opposite point of view, so as to impose their opinions indirectly, is called dialectic, in other words, heads I win and tails you lose, dressed up to look scholarly.

If I shout:

Ideal, Ideal, Ideal

Knowledge, Knowledge, Knowledge,

Boomboom, Boomboom, Boomboom

I have recorded fairly accurately Progress, Law, Morals, and all the other magnificent qualities that various very intelligent people have discussed in so many books in order, finally, to say that even so everyone has danced according to his own personal boomboom, and that he's right about his boomboom: the satisfaction of unhealthy curiosity; private bell-ringing for inexplicable needs; bath; pecuniary difficulties; a stomach with repercussions on to life; the authority of the mystical baton formulated as the grand finale of a phantom orchestra with mute bows, lubricated by philtres with a basis of animal ammonia. With the blue monocle of an angel they have dug out its interior for twenty sous worth of unanimous gratitude. ☆ If all of them are right, and if all pills are only Pink, let's try for once not to be right. ☆ People think they can explain rationally, by means of thought, what they write. But it's very relative. Thought is a fine thing for philosophy, but it's relative. Psychoanalysis is a dangerous disease, it deadens man's anti-real inclinations and systematises the bourgeoisie. There is no ultimate Truth. Dialectics is an amusing machine that leads us (in banal fashion) to the opinions which we would have held in any case. Do people really think that, by the meticulous subtlety of logic, they have demonstrated the truth and established the accuracy of their opinions? Even if logic were confirmed by the senses it would still be an organic disease. To this element, philosophers like to add: The power of observation. But this magnificent quality of the mind is precisely the proof of its impotence. People observe, they look at things from one or several points of view, they choose them from amongst the millions that exist. Experience too is the result of chance and of individual abilities. ☆ Science revolts me when it becomes a speculative system and loses its utilitarian character — which is so useless — but is at least individual. I hate slimy objectivity, and harmony, the science that considers that everything is always in order. Carry on, children, humanity ... Science says that we are nature's servants: everything is in order, make both love and war. Carry on, children, humanity, nice kind bourgeois and virgin journalists ... ☆ I am against systems; the most acceptable system is that of having none on no principle. ☆ To complete oneself, to perfect oneself in one's own pettiness to the point of filling the little vase of oneself with oneself, even the courage to fight for and against thought, all this can suddenly infernally propel us into the mystery of daily bread and the lilies of the economic field.

DADAIST SPONTANEITY

What I call the I-don't-give-a-damn attitude of life is when everyone minds his own business, at the same time as he knows how to respect other individualities, and even how to stand up for himself, the two-step becoming a national anthem, a junk shop, the wireless (the wire-less telephone) transmitting Bach fugues, illuminated advertisements and placards for brothels, the organ broadcasting carnations for God, all this at the same time, and in real terms, replacing photography and unilateral catechism.

Active simplicity.

The incapacity to distinguish between degrees of light: licking the twilight and floating in the huge mouth filled with honey and excrement. Measured against the scale of Eternity, every action is vain — (if we allow thought to have an adventure whose result would be infinitely grotesque — an important factor in the awareness of human incapacity). But if life is a bad joke, with neither goal nor initial accouchement, and because we believe we ought, like clean chrysanthemums, to make the best of a bad bargain, we have declared that the only basis of understanding is: art. It hasn't the importance that we, old hands at the spiritual, have been lavishing on it for centuries. Art does nobody any harm, and those who are capable of taking an interest in it will not only receive caresses, but also a marvellous chance to people the country of their conversation. Art is a private thing, the artist makes it for himself; a comprehensible work is the product of a journalist, and because at this moment I enjoy mixing this monster in oil paints: a paper tube imitating the metal that you press and automatically squeeze out hatred, cowardice and villainy. The artist, or the poet, rejoices in the venom of this mass condensed into one shopwalker of this trade, he is glad to be insulted, it proves his immutability. The author or the artist praised by the papers observes that his work has been understood: a miserable lining to a coat that is of public utility; rags covering brutishness, horse-piss collaborating with the heat of an animal incubating the baser insticts. Flabby, insipid flesh multiplying itself with the aid of typographical microbes.

We have done violence to the snivelling tendencies in our natures. Every infiltration of this sort is macerated diarrhoea. To encourage this sort of art is to digest it. What we need are strong, straightforward, precise works which will be forever misunderstood. Logic is a complication. Logic is always false. It draws the superficial threads of concepts and words towards illusory conclusions and centres. Its chains kill, an enormous myriapod that asphyxiates independence. If it were married to logic, art would be living in incest, engulfing, swallowing its own tail, which still belongs to its body, fornicating in itself, and temperament would become a nightmare tarred and feathered with protestantism, a monument, a mass of heavy, greyish intestines.

But suppleness, enthusiasm and even the joy of injustice, that little truth that we practise as innocents and that makes us beautiful: we are cunning, and our fingers are malleable and glide like the

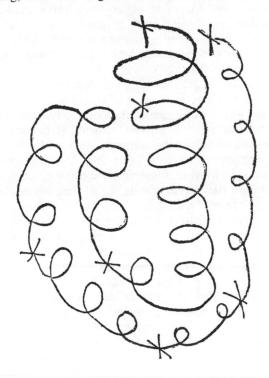

branches of that insidious and almost liquid plant; this injustice is the indication of our soul, say the cynics. This is also a point of view; but all flowers aren't saints, luckily, and what is divine in us is the awakening of anti-human action. What we are talking about here is a paper flower for the buttonhole of gentlemen who frequent the ball of masked life, the kitchen of grace, our white, lithe or fleshy girl cousins. They make a profit out of what we have selected. The contradiction and unity of opposing poles at the same time may be true. If we are absolutely determined to utter this platitude, the appendix of a libidinous, evil-smelling morality. Morals have an atrophying effect, like every other pestilential product of the intelligence. Being governed by morals and logic has made it impossible for us to be anything other than impassive towards policemen — the cause of slavery — putrid rats with whom the bourgeois are fed up to the teeth, and who have infected the only corridors of clear and clean glass that remained open to artists.

Every man must shout: there is great destructive, negative work to be done. To sweep, to clean. The cleanliness of the individual materialises after we've gone through folly, the aggressive, complete folly of a world left in the hands of bandits who have demolished and destroyed the centuries. With neither aim nor plan, without organisation: uncontrollable folly, decomposition. Those who are strong in word or in strength will survive, because they are quick to defend themselves; the agility of their limbs and feelings flames on their faceted flanks.

Morals have given rise to charity and pity, two dumplings that have grown like elephants, planets, which people call good. There is nothing good about them. Goodness is lucid, clear and resolute, and ruthless towards compromise and politics. Morality infuses chocolate into every man's veins. This task is not ordained by a supernatural force, but by a trust of ideas-merchants and academic monopolists. Sentimentality: seeing a group of bored and quarrelling men, they invented the calendar and wisdom as a remedy. By sticking labels on to things, the battle of the philosophers was let loose (money-grubbing, mean and meticulous weights and measures) and one understood once again that pity is a feeling, like diarrhoea in relation to disgust, that undermines health, the filthy carrion job of jeopardising the sun. I proclaim the opposition of all the cosmic faculties to that blennorrhoea of a putrid sun that issues from the factories of philosophical thought, the fight to the death, with all the resources of

DADAIST DISGUST

Every product of disgust that is capable of becoming a negation of the family is *dada*; protest with the fists of one's whole being in destructive action: **DADA**; acquaintance with all the means hitherto rejected by the sexual prudishness of easy compromise and good manners: **DADA**; abolition of logic, dance of those who are incapable of creation: **DADA**; every hierarchy and social equation established for values by our valets: DADA; every object, all objects, feelings and obscurities, every apparition and the precise shock of parallel lines, are means for the battle of: **DADA**; the abolition of memory: **DADA**; the abolition of archaeology: **DADA** the abolition of prophets: **DADA**; the abolition of the future: DADA; the absolute and indiscutable belief in every god that is an immediate product of spontaneity: **DADA**; the elegant and unprejudiced leap from one harmony to another sphere; the trajectory of a word, a cry, thrown into the air like an acoustic disc; to respect all individualities in their folly of the moment, whether serious, fearful, timid, ardent, vigorous, decided or enthusiastic; to strip one's church of every useless and unwieldy accessory; to spew out like a luminous cascade any offensive or loving thought, or to cherish it – with the lively satisfaction that it's all precisely the same thing – with the same intensity in the bush, which is free of insects for the blue-blooded, and gilded with the bodies of archangels, with one's soul. Liberty: **DADA DADA DADA**; — the roar of contorted pains, the interweaving of contraries and of all contradictions, freaks and irrelevancies: LIFE.

III

UNPRETENTIOUS PROCLAMATION

Art is putting itself to sleep to bring about the birth of the new world **"ART"** — *a parrot word* — replaced by **DADA, PLESIOSAURUS,** or handkerchief

The talent THAT CAN BE LEARNT *turns the poet into an ironmonger* TODAY *criticism balances doesn't throw up any resemblances*

Hypertrophic painters hyperaestheticised and hypnotised by the hyacinths of the muezzins of hypocritical appearance

CONSOLIDATE THE EXACT HARVEST OF CALCULATION

HYPODROME OF IMMORTAL GUARANTEES: *There is no importance there is neither transparence nor appearance*

MUSICIANS SMASH YOUR BLIND INSTRUMENTS
on the stage

The BAZOOKA *is only for my understanding.* **I write because it's natural like I piss like I'm ill**

Art needs an operation

Art is a *PRETENSION* heated at the **TIMIDITY** of the urinary basin, hysteria born in the **studio**

We are looking for a **straightforward pure sober unique** force.we are looking for **NOTHING** we affirm the **VITALITY** of every **instant** the **the anti-philosophy of** spontaneous **acrobatics**

At this moment I hate the man who whispers before the interval — eau de cologne — sour theatre. SWEET WIND.

IF EVERYONE SAYS THE OPPOSITE IT'S BECAUSE HE'S RIGHT

Prepare the action of the geyser of our blood — the submarine formation of transchromatic aeroplanes,

metals with cells and ciphered in the upsurge of images

above   the   rules   of   the

Beautiful and of its inspection

It isn't for those abortions who still worship their own navels

IV

MANIFESTO
OF MONSIEUR AA
THE ANTIPHILOSOPHER

---

without the pursuit of I worship you
which is a French boxer
maritime values as irregular as the depression of Dada in the blood
of a bicephalous animal
I glide between death and the vague phosphates that scratch
slightly at the common brain of dadaist poets
luckily
because
gold
mine
tariffs and the high cost of living have made me Decide to abandon
D's
it isn't true that sham dadas have Deprived me of them because
the Deed of reimbursement will soon be drafted
here's enough to bewail the nothing that is called nothing
and I've cleared illnesses at the customs
I the carapace and umbrella of the brain from noon till two o'clock
two hours' subscription
superstitious releasing the mechanism
of the spermatozoon ballet that you'll find being dress-rehearsed in
all the hearts of suspect individuals
I'll eat your fingers a bit
I'm renewing your subscription to the celluloid love that creaks like

metal gates
and you are idiots
I shall come back once in the guise of your renascent urine as the obstetric wind of joie de vivre
and I'm going to establish a boarding school for poets' supporters
and I've come again to start again
and you're all idiots
and the selfkleptomaniac's key only works with crepuscular oil on every knot of every machine there's the nose of a new-born baby
and we're all idiots
and very suspect of a new form of intelligence and a new logic after our own manner
which isn't at all Dada

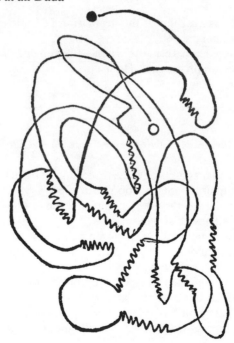

and you're letting yourselves be led astray by Aaism
and you're all idiots
poultices
of the surgical spirit of purified sleep
of bandages
and of virgin
idiots

TRISTAN TZARA

Have a good look at me!
I'm an idiot, I'm a practical joker, I'm a hoaxer.
Have a good look at me!
I'm ugly, my face has no expression, I'm small.
I'm like all the rest of you![1]
But ask yourselves, before you look at me, whether the iris by which you dispatch arrows of liquid sentiments isn't in fact fly-shit, if your belly's eyes are not sections of tumours whose looks will at one moment emerge from some part of your body in the form of a blennorrhagic discharge.
You see with your navels – why do you hide from your navels the ridiculous spectacle we offer them? And lower down, women's genitals, with teeth, that swallow everything — the poetry of eternity, love, pure love, naturally — rare steaks and oil painting. Everybody who looks and who understands can easily be classified somewhere between poetry and love, between steak and painting. They'll be digested, they'll be digested. I was recently accused of the theft of some furs. Probably because people thought I should still be classified as a poet. One of those poets who satisfy their legitimate need of cold onania in hot furs: *H a H u*, I know other, equally platonic, pleasures. Ring up your family on the telephone

---

[1] I wanted to give myself a bit of publicity.

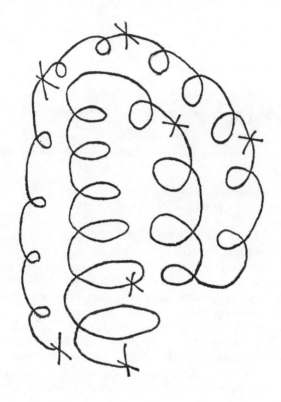

and piss down the hole designed for musical, gastronomic and sacred nonsense.

DADA suggests 2 solutions:

NO MORE LOOKS!
NO MORE WORDS![2]

[2] No more manifestos.

Stop looking!
Stop talking!

For I, chameleon alteration infiltration with convenient attitudes —
multicoloured opinions for every occasion size and price — I do
the opposite of what I recommend to other people.[3]

I've forgotten something:

where ? why ? how ?
in other words:
the ventilator of cold examples will serve the fragile snake of the
procession and I have never had the pleasure of seeing you, my
dear, the ear will take itself out of the envelope rigid like all marine
equipment and the products of Aa & Co's firm, chewing-gum for
example and dogs have blue eyes, I drink camomile tea, they drink
the wind, DADA introduces new points of view, people sit down
now at the corners of tables, in attitudes which lean a bit to the left
and to the right, that's why I've quarrelled with Dada, insist
everywhere on the suppression of the Ds, eat Aa, brush yourself
with Aa toothpaste, buy your clothes at Aa's. Aa is a handkerchief
and genitals blowing their noses rapid collapse — made of rubber
— noiseless, needs neither manifestos nor address books, it gives a
25% discount buy your clothes at Aa's he has blue eyes.

[3] Sometimes.

VI

MONSIEUR AA
THE ANTIPHILOSOPHER
SENDS US
THIS MANIFESTO

Long live the undertakers of the combine!
Every act is a cerebral revolver shot — both the insignificant
gesture and the decisive movement are attacks (I open the fan of
knock-outs for the distillation of the air that separates us) — and
with the words put down on paper I enter, solemnly, into myself.
In the scalp of notions I implant my 60 fingers and brutally shake
the curtains, the teeth, the bolts of their joints
I shut, I open, I spit. Careful! The moment has come when I should
tell you that I've been lying. If there is a system in the lack of
system — that of my proportions — I never apply it.
In other words, I lie. I lie when I apply it, I lie when I don't apply it,
I lie when I write that I lie because I do not lie — because I have
lived the mirror of my father — chosen from the profits of baccarat
— from town to town — for myself has never been myself — for
the saxophone wears like a rose the assassination of the visceral
car-driver — he's made of sexual copper and the leaves of
racecourses. Thus drummed the maize, the alarm and pellagra
where the matches grow.

Extermination. Yes, naturally.
But doesn't exist. Myself: mixture kitchen theatre. Long live the
stretcher-bearers of the convocations of ecstasies!

Lying is ecstasy — which lasts longer than a second — there is nothing that lasts longer. Idiots brood over the century — they start all over again several centuries later — idiots remain within the circle for ten years — idiots hover over the dial of a year — Myself (an idiot) I stay there for five minutes.

The claim of the blood to distribute in my body and my event the accident of colour of the first woman I touched with my eyes in these tentacular times. The bitterest banditry is to finish one's thought-out phrase. The banditry of the gramophone, the little anti-human mirage that I like in myself — because I believe it to be ridiculous and dishonest. But the bankers of language will always get their little percentage on the discussion. The presence of (at least) one boxer is indispensable for a match — affiliated members of a gang of dadaist assassins have signed a self-protection contract for operations of this sort. Their number is extremely limited — the presence of (at least) one singer for a duet, of (at least) one signatory for a receipt, of (at least) one eye for sight, being absolutely indispensable.

Put the photographic plate of the face in the acid bath.

The shocks that have sensitised it will become visible and will surprise you.

Punch yourself in the face and drop dead.

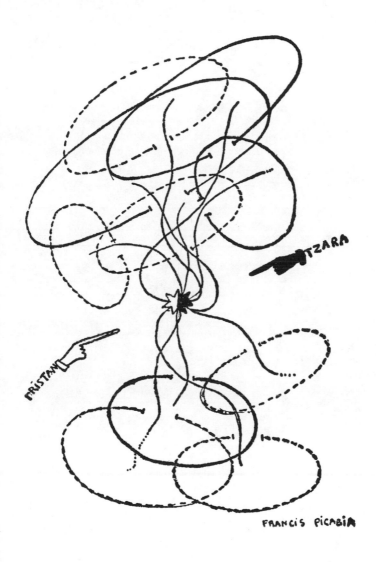

VII

DADA
MANIFESTO
ON FEEBLE LOVE AND
BITTER LOVE

I

preamble = sardanapalus
one = suitcase
woman = women
trousers = water
if = moustache
2 = three
stick = perhaps
after = sightreading
irritant = emerald
vice = screw
october = periscope
nerve = 🖝

or all this together in any old savoury, soapy, brusque or definitive order — drawn by lot — is alive.
It is thus that over and above the vigilant spirit of the clergyman built at the corner of every road, be it animal, vegetable, imaginable or organic, everything is the same as everything that is not the same. Even if I didn't believe it, it's the truth of the fact that I've put it on paper — because it's a lie that I have FIXED like a butterfly on a hat.

31

Lies circulate — welcome Mister Opportune and Mister Convenient: I arrest them — they're turning into the truth.

Thus DADA takes on the job of the two-wheeled cops and of undercover morality.

Everyone (at a certain moment) was sound in mind and body. Repeat this 30 times.

I consider myself very likeable.

Tristan Tzara

II

A manifesto is a communication made to the whole world, whose only pretension is to the discovery of an instant cure for political, astronomical, artistic, parliamentary, agronomical and literary syphilis. It may be pleasant, and good-natured, it's always right, it's strong, vigorous and logical.

Apropos of logic, I consider myself very likeable.

Tristan Tzara

Pride is the star that yawns and penetrates through the eyes and the mouth, she insists, strikes deep, on her breast is inscribed: you will die. This is her only remedy. Who still believes in doctors? I prefer the poet who is a fart in a steam-engine — he's gentle but he doesn't cry — polite and semi-homosexual, he floats. I don't give a single damn about either of them. It's by pure (unnecessary) chance that the first should be German and the second Spanish. Far be it from us, in actual fact, the idea of discovering the theory of the probability of races and the epistolary perfection of bitterness.

III

We have always made mistakes, but the greatest mistakes are the poems we have written. Gossip has one single raison d'être: the rejuvenation and maintenance of biblical traditions. Gossip is encouraged by the administration of the post office which, alas! is perfecting itself, encouraged by the state-controlled tobacco company, the railways, the hospitals, the undertaking industry and cloth factories. Gossip is encouraged by the culture of the family. Gossip is encouraged by Peter's pence. Every drop of saliva that escapes from a conversation is converted into gold. Since the people have always needed divinities to protect the three essential laws, which are those of God: eating, making love and shitting, since the kings are on their travels and the laws are too hard, the only thing that counts at the moment is gossip. The form under which it most often appears is DADA.

There are some people (journalists, lawyers, amateurs, philosophers) who even think that other forms: business, marriages, visits, wars, various conferences, limited companies, politics, accidents, dance halls, economic crises, fits of hysterics, are variations of dada.

Not being an imperialist, I don't share their opinion — I believe, rather, that dada is only a divinity of the second order, which must quite simply be placed beside the other forms of the new mechanism of the religions of the interregnum.

Is simplicity simple, or dada?

I consider myself rather likeable.

Tristan Tzara

IV

Is poetry necessary? I know that those who shout loudest against it are actually preparing a comfortable perfection for it; they call it the Future Hygienic.

People envisage the (ever-impending) annihilation of art. Here they are looking for a more art-like art. Hygiene becomes mygod mygod purity.

Must we no longer believe in words? Since when do they express the contrary of what the organ that utters them thinks and wants? * Herein lies the great secret:

Thought is made in the mouth.

I still consider myself very likeable.

Tristan Tzara

A great Canadian philosopher said: Thought and the past are also very likeable.

* Thinks, wants, and wishes to think.

V

A friend, who is too good a friend of mine not to be very intelligent, said to me the other day:

a shudder **IS ONLY THE**
a palmist
WAY PEOPLE SAY good morning **AND**
good evening
WHICH DEPENDS ON THE FORM
THAT HAS BEEN GIVEN
TO its forget-me-not
his hair

I answered

YOU ARE RIGHT idiot **BECAUSE I AM**
prince
CONVINCED OF THE contrary
Tartary
naturally **WE ARE NOT (DO NOT)**
we hesitate
right. I am called **THE OTHER**
wish to understand

Since diversity is diverting, this game of golf gives the illusion of a "certain" depth. I support all the conventions — to suppress them would be to make new ones, which would complicate our lives in a truly repugnant fashion.

We wouldn't know any more what is fashionable: to love the children of the first or the second marriage. The "pistil of the pistol" has often landed us in bizarre and restless situations. *To disorder* meanings — *to disorder* notions and all the little tropical rains of *demoralisation, disorganisation, destruction* and *billiard-breaks*, are actions which are insured against lightning and recognised as being of public utility. There is one known fact: dadaists are only to be found these days in the French Academy. I nevertheless consider myself very likeable.

Tristan Tzara

VI

It seems that this exists: more logical, very logical, too logical, less
logical, not very logical, really logical, fairly logical.
Well then, draw the inferences.
"I have."
Now think of the person you love most.
"Have you?"
Tell me the number and I'll tell you the lottery.

VII

A priori, in other words with its eyes closed, Dada places before action and above all: *Doubt*. *DADA* doubts everything. Dada is an armadillo. Everything is Dada, too. Beware of Dada.

Anti-dadaism is a disease: selfkleptomania, man's normal condition, is DADA.
But the real dadas are against DADA.

The selfkleptomaniac.

The person who steals — without thinking of his own interests, or of his will — elements of his individual, is a kleptomaniac. He steals himself. He causes the characters that alienate him from the community to disappear. The bourgeois resemble one another — they're all alike. They used not to be alike. They have been taught to steal — stealing has become a function — the most convenient and least dangerous thing is to steal oneself. They are all very poor. The poor are against DADA. They have a lot to do with their brains. They'll never get to the end of it. They work. They work on themselves — deceive themselves — they steal themselves — they are very poor. Poor things. The poor work. The poor are against DADA. He who is against DADA is for me, a famous man said, but then he died. They buried him like a true dadaist. Anno domini Dada. Beware! And remember this example.

VIII

TO MAKE A DADAIST POEM

Take a newspaper.
Take some scissors.
Choose from this paper an article of the length you want to make
your poem.
Cut out the article.
Next carefully cut out each of the words that makes up this article
and put them all in a bag.
Shake gently.
Next take out each cutting one after the other.
Copy conscientiously in the order in which they left the bag.
The poem will resemble you.
And there you are — an infinitely original author of charming
sensibility, even though unappreciated by the vulgar herd. *

---

* *Example:*
when dogs cross the air in a diamond like ideas and the appendix of
the meninx tells the time of the alarm programme (the title is mine)
prices they are yesterday suitable next pictures/ appreciate the
dream era of the eyes/ pompously that to recite the gospel sort
darkens/ group apotheosis imagine said he fatality power of
colours/ carved flies (in the theatre) flabbergasted reality a delight/
spectator all to effort of the no more 10 to 12/ during divagation
twirls descends pressure/ render some mad single-file flesh on a
monstrous crushing stage/ celebrate but their 160 adherents in
steps on put on my nacreous/ sumptuous of land bananas
sustained illuminate/ joy ask together almost/ of has the a such that
the invoked visions/ some sings latter laughs/ exits situation
disappears describes she 25 dance bows/ dissimulated the whole of
it isn't was/ magnificent ascent has the band better light whose
lavishness stage music-halls me/ reappears following instant moves
live/ business he didn't has lent/ manner words come these people

IX

There are some people who explain, because there are others who learn. Abolish them and all that's left is dada.

Dip your pen into a black liquid with manifesto intentions — it's only your autobiography that you're hatching under the belly of the flowering cerebellum.

Biography is the paraphernalia of the famous man. Great or strong. And there *you* are, a simple man like the rest of them, once you've dipped your pen into the ink, full of

PRETENSIONS

which manifest themselves in forms as diverse as they are unforeseen, which apply to every form of activity and of state of mind and of mimicry: There you are, full of

AMBITIONS

to keep yourself on the dial of life, in the place where you've only just arrived, to proceed along the illusory and ridiculous upward path towards an apotheosis that only exists in your neurasthenia: there you are, full of

PRIDE

greater, stronger, more profound than all the others.

Dear colleagues: a great man, a little one, a strong, weak, profound, superficial one,

that's why you're all going to die.

There are some people who have antedated their manifestos to make other people believe that they had the idea of their own greatness a little earlier. My dear colleagues: before after, past future, now yesterday,

that's why you're going to die.

There are some people who have said: dada is good because it isn't bad, dada is bad, dada is a religion, dada is a poem, dada is a spirit, dada is sceptical, dada is magic, I know dada.

My dear colleagues: good bad, religion poetry, spirit scepticism,

definition definition,
that's why you're all going to die,
and you *will* die, I promise you.
The great mystery is a secret, but it's known to a few people. They will never say what dada is. To amuse you once again I'll tell you something like:
dada is the dictatorship of the spirit, or
dada is the dictatorship of language,
or else
dada is the death of the spirit,
which will please many of my friends. Friends.

X

It is certain that since Gambetta, the war, Panama and the Steinheil affair, intelligence is to be found in the street. The intelligent man has become an all-round, normal person. What we lack, what has some interest, what is rare because he has the anomalies of a precious being, the freshness and liberty of the great antimen, is

THE IDIOT

Dada is working with all its might towards the universal installation of the idiot. But consciously. And tends itself to become more and more of one.

Dada is terrible: it doesn't feel sorry about the defeats of intelligence.

Dada could rather be called cowardly, but cowardly like a mad dog; it recognises neither method nor persuasive excess.

The lack of garters which makes it systematically bend down reminds us of the famous lack of system which basically has never existed. The false rumour was started by a laundress at the bottom of her page, the page was taken to the barbaric country where humming-birds act as the sandwich-men of cordial nature.

This was told me by a watch-maker who was holding a supple syringe which, in characteristic memory of the hot countries, he called phlegmatic and insinuating.

XI

Dada is a dog — a compass — the lining of the stomach — neither new nor a nude Japanese girl — a gasometer of jangled feelings — Dada is brutal and doesn't go in for propaganda — Dada is a quantity of life in transparent, effortless and gyratory transformation.

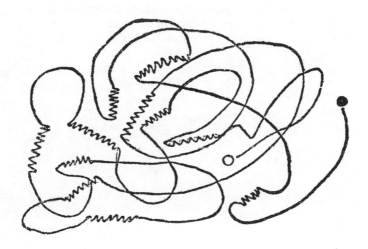

gentlemen and ladies buy come in and buy and don't read you'll see the fellow who has in his hands the key to niagara the man with a game leg in the game box his hemispheres in a suitcase his nose enclosed in a chinese lantern you'll see you'll see you'll see the belly dance in the massachusetts saloon the fellow who sticks the nail in and the tyre goes down mademoiselle atlantide's silk stockings the trunk that goes 6 times round the world to find the addressee monsieur and his fiancée his brother and his sister-in-law you'll find the carpenter's address the toad-watch the nerve like a paper-knife you'll have the address of the minor pin for the feminine sex and that of the fellow who supplies the obscene photos to the king of greece as well as the address of *l'action française*.

XIII

DADA is a virgin microbe
DADA is against the high cost of living
DADA
limited company for the exploitation of ideas
DADA has 391 different attitudes and colours according to the sex of the president
It changes — affirms — says the opposite at the same time — no importance — shouts — goes fishing.
Dada is the chameleon of rapid and self-interested change.
Dada is against the future. Dada is dead. Dada is absurd. Long live Dada. Dada is not a literary school, howl

Tristan Tzara

XIV

To "prettify" life in the lorgnette — a blanket of caresses — a panoply with butterflies — *that's the life of life's chambermaids.*

To sleep on a razor and on fleas in rut — to travel in a barometer — to piss like a cartridge — to make faux pas, be idiotic, take showers of holy minutes — be beaten, always be the last one — shout out the opposite of what the other fellow says — be the editorial office and the bathroom of God who every day takes a bath in us in company with the cesspool clearer — *that's the life of dadaists.*

To be intelligent — respect everyone — die on the field of honour — subscribe to the Loan — vote for So-and-So — respect for nature and painting — to barrack at dada manifestations — *that's the life of men.*

XV

DADA is not a doctrine to be put into practice: Dada — is for lying: a successful business. Dada gets into debt and doesn't live on its well-filled wallet. The good Lord created a universal language, that's why people don't take him seriously. A language is a utopia. God can allow himself not to be successful: so can Dada. That's why the critics say: Dada goes in for luxuries, or Dada is in rut. God goes in for luxuries, or God is in rut. Who's right: God, Dada or the critic?

"You're deviating," a charming reader tells me.

— No no, not at all! I simply wanted to reach the conclusion: Subscribe to Dada, the only loan that doesn't pay.

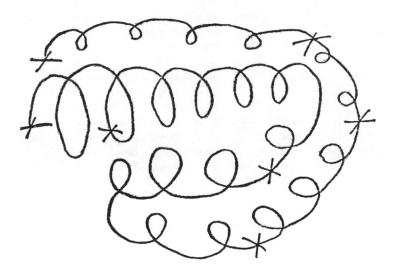

XVI

howl howl howl howl howl howl howl howl
howl howl howl howl howl howl howl howl
howl howl howl howl howl howl howl howl
howl howl howl howl howl howl howl howl
howl howl howl howl howl howl howl howl
howl howl howl howl howl howl howl howl
howl howl howl howl howl howl howl howl
howl howl howl howl howl howl howl howl
howl howl howl howl howl howl howl howl
howl howl howl howl howl howl howl howl
howl howl howl howl howl howl howl howl
howl howl howl howl howl howl howl howl
howl howl howl howl howl howl howl howl
howl howl howl howl howl howl howl howl
howl howl howl howl howl howl howl howl
howl howl howl howl howl howl howl howl
howl howl howl howl howl howl howl howl
howl howl howl howl howl howl howl howl
howl howl howl howl howl howl howl howl
howl howl howl howl howl howl howl howl
howl howl howl howl howl howl howl howl
howl howl howl howl howl howl howl howl
howl howl howl howl howl howl howl howl
howl howl howl howl howl howl howl howl
howl howl howl howl howl howl howl howl

Who still considers himself very likeable

Tristan Tzara

APPENDIX
HOW I BECAME
CHARMING
LIKEABLE AND
DELIGHTFUL

I sleep very late. I commit suicide at 65%. My life is very cheap, it's only 30% of life for me. My life has 30% of life. It lacks arms, strings and a few buttons. 5% is devoted to a state of semi-lucid stupor accompanied by anaemic crackling. This 5% is called DADA. So life is cheap. Death is a bit more expensive. But life is charming and death is equally charming.

A few days ago I was at a meeting of imbeciles. There were a lot of people there. Everyone was charming. Tristan Tzara, a small, absurd and insignificant individual was giving a lecture on the art of becoming charming. He was charming, at that. Everyone is charming. And witty. It's delightful, isn't it? Everyone is delightful, at that. 9 degrees below zero. It's charming, isn't it? No, it isn't charming. God isn't up to it. He isn't even in the directory. But even so he's charming.

Ambassadors, poets, counts, princes, musicians, journalists, actors, writers, diplomats, directors, dressmakers, socialists, princesses and baronesses are charming.

You're all of you charming, very subtle, witty and delightful. Tristan Tzara says to you: he's quite willing to do something else, but he prefers to remain an idiot, a practical joker and a hoaxer. Be sincere for a moment: what I've just said to you — is it charming or idiotic?

49

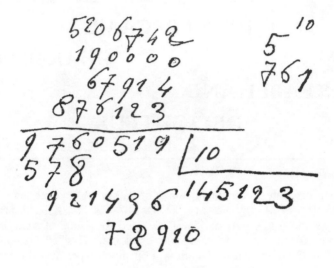

There are some people (journalists, lawyers, amateurs, philosophers) who even think that business, marriages, visits, wars, various conferences, limited companies, politics, accidents, dance halls, economic crises, fits of hysterics, are variations of dada.

Not being an imperialist, I don't share their opinion. I believe, rather, that dada is only a divinity of the second order, which must quite simply be placed beside the other forms of the new mechanism of the religions of the interregnum.

Is simplicity simple, or dada?

I consider myself rather likeable.

Tristan Tzara

COLONIAL
SYLLOGISM

No one can escape fate
No one can escape DADA

Only DADA can make you escape fate.

You owe me 943 francs 50

No more drunkards!
No more aeroplanes!
No more vigour!
No more urinary passages!
No more enigmas!

Lampisteries

TRANSLATOR'S NOTE:

A lampiste is a man who makes lamps.
He is also in *argot* a scapegoat.

note on art

Art is at present the only self-contained construction about which there is no more to be said, such is its richness, vitality, meaning and wisdom. To understand, to see. To describe a flower: relative poetry more or less artificial flower. To see.

Until we discover the intimate vibrations of the final cell of a mathematical god-brain and the explanation of the primary astronomies — its essence — we shall always find ourselves describing this impossibility with its logical elements of perpetual contradiction, a marshland of stars and of futile bell-ringing. Like toads squatting on cold lanterns, squashing the descriptive intelligence of the red belly. What people write on art is an educative work, and in this sense it has a right to exist. We want to give back to mankind the ability to understand that a unique fraternity comes into existence at the intense moment when beauty and life itself, brought into high tension on a wire, ascend towards a flash-point; the blue tremor linked to the ground by our magnetised gaze which covers the peak with snow. The miracle. I open my heart to creation.

There are many artists who are no longer looking for solutions in the object and in its relations with the outside world; they are cosmic or primary, decided, simple, wise and serious.

The diversity of today's artists is a compressed jet of water scattered at crystal liberty. And their efforts create new limpid organisms, in a world of purity, with the aid of transparencies and of the materiality of construction of a simple image which is in the process of formation. They are carrying on the tradition; the past and its evolution are pushing them slowly, like a snake, towards their inner, direct consequences, beyond both surfaces and reality.

note on negro art

The new art is first and foremost concentration, the lines from the base to the apex of a pyramid forming a cross; through purity we have first deformed and then decomposed the object, we have approached its surface, we have penetrated it. We want a clarity that is direct. Art is grouped into camps, each with its special skills, within its own frontiers. The influences of a foreign nature which were mixed up in it are the rags of a Renaissance lining still sticking to the souls of our fellow men, for my brother's soul has sharp branches, black with autumn.

My other brother is naive and good, and laughs. He eats in Africa or along the South Sea Islands. He concentrates his vision on the head, carves it out of wood that is as hard as iron, patiently, without bothering about the conventional relationship between the head and the rest of the body. What he thinks is: man walks vertically, everything in nature is symmetrical. While working, new relationships organise themselves according to degree of necessity; this is how the expression of purity came into being.

From blackness, let us extract light. Simple, rich luminous naivety. Different materials, the scales of form. To construct in balanced hierarchy. EYE: button, open wide, round, and pointed, to penetrate my bones and my belief. Transform my country into a prayer of joy or anguish. Cotton wool eye, flow in my blood.

Art, in the infancy of time, was prayer. Wood and stone were truth. In man I see the moon, plants, blackness, metal, stars, fish. Let the cosmic elements glide symmetrically. Deform, boil. Hands are big and strong. Mouths contain the power of darkness, invisible substance, goodness, fear, wisdom, creation, fire.

No one has seen so clearly as I this dark grinding whiteness.

note on art
h. arp

Having finally succeeded in making parallel lines meet at infinity, and arrived at the sobriety of skilful superimpositions, he shook his art like a thousand-branched explosion whose richness of forms and allusions are marvellously grouped in one simple organic unity.

The summit sings what is being spoken in the depths.

Nature is organised in its totality, the rigging of the fabulous ship up to the focal point in the principles that regulate crystals and insects in hierarchies like trees.

Every natural thing keeps its clarity of organisation, hidden, pulled by relationships which are grouped together like the family of lunar lights, the hub of a wheel that might revolve ad infinitum, the sphere, it ties its liberty, its final, absolute existence, to innumerable and constructive laws.

My sister, root, flower, stone.

The organism is complete in the mute intelligence of a nervure and in its appearance.

Man is dirty, he kills animals, plants, his brothers, he quarrels, he's intelligent, talks too much, doesn't know how to express his thoughts.

But the artist is a creator: he knows how to work in a manner that becomes organic. He decides. He makes man better. Cultivates the garden of intentions. Commands.
The purity of a principle makes me happy. To see, beyond the horizontal which expands as it tranquillises the vegetable novelties of far-off countries, icy inflorescences.

The vertical: thinking of infinity while feeling the depth of a moment of animality.

H. Arp
Symmetry
flower of a midnight encounter
in which fever and bird become the tranquillity of a halo
and the hop-bine climbs
the flower becomes crystal or beetle magnet star
to want to live a simple life.

If we can live a miracle we have reached the level where your blood will be an order of archangels, the medicine of astronomy, reader, — belief stored up clearly in simple hearts, — wisdom, knowledge.

guillaume apollinaire
"le poète assassiné"
"les mamelles de tirésias"

For this poet, life is a serious and revolving game of jokes, sadness, good-nature, naivety and modernism, turn and turn about. The finger bores into all sorts of flesh till it gets to the innermost part that shrieks and vibrates, where it becomes a flower, and laughs. The unforeseen is everywhere's explosive star, and speed harmonises with the tranquil, curious narrator, in a natural affirmation of constant novelty. This collision begets the burlesque. The past put in a reflecting mirror which is projected several centuries ahead. With the unerringness of a cowboy. With an elegant and grotesque turn. Impulsive, capricious, subtle. At the gallop above life, man is ridiculous.

While Second Lieutenant Apollinaire was in hospital with a serious head-wound, his book of stories, *Le poète assassiné* appeared, and the Croniamantal poet in a frock coat, in a pink cradle, burst forth simultaneously in Munich and in various cellars frequented by princes.

The theatre. Since it still remains attached to a romantic imitation of life, to an illogical fiction, let us give it all the natural vigour that it had at the outset: whether it be entertainment or poetry.

61

The tortured little sensitivities of changeable psychologies, a declamatory theory, cannot reveal a truth that will for ever remain obscure, like all useless actions and their relative results.

At an evening organised by the review *Sic* on June 24th, Apollinaire's surrealist drama *Les mamelles de Tirésias* was performed. Let women have children — their duty and their purpose. It's reasonable and correct.

It seems that people enjoyed themselves very much listening to what Apollinaire said so clearly in sets made out of scraps of newspapers and in masks which were supposed to represent fever cut out of the margin of a supreme, multicoloured star. Laughter is men's goodness.

Look for medicines and wisdom in songs, and let's start again.

pierre reverdy
"le voleur de talan"

An unexpected book, almost the novel of one's dreams. Since the Renaissance, the centre and principle of art has been anecdote: in other words, a story told to a rich man in order to awaken in him a "feeling"; 64% pity and the rest humility, etc., + the forgetting of an inconvenient instant in which we made a splendid bargain. Half of all writers know this and take advantage of it; the other half are still trying to warm up the egg of anecdote to turn it into art, they are speculating on the short tradition of a few centuries. But they serve the same stomach, which they neither wanted nor foresaw.

The Renaissance was the infernal age of the cynic. For art it was a shambles, divided between anecdote and charm. Illusion became the goal, and man was trying to go one better than God. But the problems of an eventful life made him interesting and, unfortunately, productive.

We want to continue the tradition of Negro, Egyptian, Byzantine and Gothic art and destroy in ourselves the atavistic sensitivity bequeathed to us by the detestable era that followed the quattrocento.

Reverdy's novel is a poem. Its episodes are carefully muffled up in a substance with which we are unfamiliar. The collision of its elements is particularly brutal. But it is a difficult life that burns within the golden egg. Straight lines emerge from this flesh, penetrate us and link us to it. For Reverdy the action, transformed into a centipede, advances slowly inside the organism of the novel, and a hundred bees bring us little by little, by thousands of invisible stings, the consequences and the facts, and introduce them uniformly into our bloodstream.

Le Voleur de Talan is above all a radiator of vibrations, and the images which are discharged in all directions (an almost electrical effect as they go past) unite around it; because of this, Reverdy's work is COSMIC. But this ambulant and ever-renewed halo leaves us with a cloudy impression and the bitter taste that man is the centre of it and that he can, in his little world, become a god-master.

What I call "cosmic" is an essential quality of a work of art. Because it implies order, which is the necessary condition of the life of every organism. Multiple, diverse and distant elements are, more or less intensely, concentrated in the work; the artist collects them, chooses them, arranges them, makes them into a construction or a composition. Order is the representation of a unity governed by those universal faculties, sobriety and the purity of precision.

There are two principles in the cosmic:
(1) To attach equal importance to each object, being, material, and organism in the universe.
(2) To stress man's importance, to group round him, in order to subordinate them to him, beings, objects, etc ...

The nucleus of the latter principle is a psychological method; the danger is the need to CORRECT men. They should be left to what they want to become — superior beings. The poet allows himself to be implicated at the whim of succession and impression. For the former principle, this need takes on a new form: to place men beside the other elements, just as they are, to make men BETTER.

To work together, anonymously, on the great cathedral of life we are preparing, to level man's instincts, for if we were to stress his personality too much, he would take on babylonian proportions of spite and cynicism.

Reverdy, in grouping breaths, and the relations of the elements, around man, creates near-material conditions which remain stagnant throughout the journeys of the various characters, and towards the end of the book, if we have been following with some care the steps covered, we almost suffocate in that atmosphere, knowing as we do the secrets of its composition. One of the great qualities of this book is that it moves us so strongly, given Reverdy's deliberate sobriety in the choice of the means that he uses; in this he is honest and serious. He comes close to the first principle in that he does not moralise, because he allows all the elements, except man, to appear simultaneously. To art for art's sake, Reverdy opposes art for life's sake. To which *we* oppose life for the sake of cosmic diversity, for totality, for the universal, and we want to see as innate in the latter the slow life which exists, and even sleeps, in what is usually called death. But theories and formulae are relative and elastic — in terms of the absolute, they would become narrow dogmas and fanaticism — and we don't want to go in for that.

Reverdy's novel must be read; its poetry is wise and calm, as if it were the evidence of a tranquillity that grows and increases in its own power. A cascade that seems to fall from on high, like a productive conflagration, a great tree with multiple and diverse fruits.

pierre albert-birot

trente et un poèmes de poche

Irregular necklaces of houses, green fir trees. Each notion in its own box: an atmosphere in a box of matches and speed captured; insects, trams, crawling up towards a glass head. To say: futurism for young ladies, an explosion in a convent school and, squashed under soft pillows, new landscapes? But each little page shouts too loudly and implodes in its vase, each one contains a new idea, and we are astrally amazed at the rapid passage (a little too brutal, but perhaps necessary) of the images of intense and highly-coloured life.

Translator's note: Pierre Albert-Birot's widow in helping with certain technical points of meaning has pointed out that this form of criticism is a *critical synthesis*, the point of which is to give an impression of the work without the critic intervening personally. The review is a form of digest in which the intelligent reader can discern the writer's opinion of the work in question.

note on negro poetry

> *"I don't even want to know that there were men before me" (DESCARTES), but some simple, essential laws, the pathetic, secret fermentation of a solid earth.*

To fix at the point where forces have accumulated, from which the expressed meaning springs, the invisible radiation of substance, the natural — though hidden and accurate — relationship, naively, without explanation.

To round off and arrange images into forms and constructions according to their weight, their colour, their matter, or organise values, material and durable densities on different spatial levels without subordinating anything to them. Classification of *opéras comiques* sanctioned by the aesthetics of the props. (O, my drawer number ABSOLUTE.)

I can't bear going into a house where the balconies, the "embellishments", are carefully stuck on to the walls. And yet the sun and the stars continue to vibrate and hum freely in space, but I am loath to identify explanatory (and probably asphyxiating) hypotheses with the principles of life, activity and certainty.

The crocodile hatches future life, rain falls for vegetable silence, we are not creators by analogy. The beauty of the satellites — the lesson of light — will content us, for we are only God for the country of our knowledge, within the laws in which we live our experience on this earth, on both sides of our equator, within our frontiers. A perfect example of the infinite that we can verify: the sphere.

To round off and arrange images into forms and constructions according to their weight, their colour, their matter, or organise values, material and durable densities by personal decision and the unshakeable strength of the sensitivity, an understanding commensurate with the matter transformed, very close to the veins and rubbing itself against them while waiting for a present and definitive joy. An organism is created when its elements are ready for life. Poetry lives primarily for the functions of the dance, of religion, of music and of work.

guillaume appollinaire is dead

He fell like the feverish "rain" that he had so carefully composed for a Paris magazine. Will the trains, the dreadnoughts, the variety theatres and the factories raise the wind of mourning for the most enduring, the most alert, the most enthusiastic of French poets? The fog isn't enough, nor is the tumult and the shouting. His season should have been the joy of victory, of *our* victory, that of the new men working in essential darkness, shaping the essential Logos. He knew the mechanism of the stars, the exact proportion of turmoil and discretion.

His spirit was a gallop of clarity, and the hail of fresh words, the escort of their crystalline kernels, were the angels.

He'll meet Henri Rousseau.

Is Apollinaire dead?

r. huelsenbeck
"prières fantastiques"

Energy and speed propelled over the glacier, vertiginous currents leaping furiously through invisible obstacles, a stagnant effervescence expanding enormously above, descending into the mines, thrusting out on all sides, always struggling and calling on all objects, colours, feelings, races, factories, animals and different languages to help him — his companions, his witnesses. He casts his vision of paradise into hell, and vice versa; nothing is sacred, everything is of divine essence. In this suspense — gymnastics in the irregular movement of the pendulum (irony, deep voice, sacrilegious flower), which gradually slows down towards the end of the book, calm and serious, clear, a wise passion, the final prayer resounds.

The representation of noise sometimes really, objectively becomes noise, and the grotesque takes on the proportions of disconnected, chaotic phrases. The bourgeois spirit, which renders ideas usable and useful, tries to assign to poetry the invisible role of the principle engine of the universal machine: the practical soul. With its help they'll give Christ back to men: expressionism. In this way it is possible to organise and fabricate everything. Liberty, fraternity, equality, expressionism, are produced. Huelsenbeck is one of the rare people who, having shouted and protested, will remain inaccessible to the paths of the snivellers disguised as butterflies.

note on poetry

The poet of the last station has given up vain weeping; lamentation slows down progress. The humidity of past ages. People who feed on tears are contented and obtuse, they thread their tears behind the necklaces of their souls so as to cheat the snakes. The poet can go in for Swedish gymnastics. But for abundance and explosion he knows how to kindle hope TODAY. Whether tranquil, ardent, furious, intimate, pathetic, slow or impetuous, his burning desire is for enthusiasm, that fecund form of intensity.

To know how to recognise and pick up the signs of the power we are awaiting, which are everywhere; in the fundamental language of cryptograms, engraved on crystals, on shells, on rails, in clouds, or in glass; inside snow, or light, or coal; on the hand, in the beams grouped round the magnetic poles, on wings.

Persistence quickens joy and shoots it like an arrow up to the celestial domes, to distil the quintessence from the waves of phlegmatic nourishment, creating new life. Flowing in all colours and bleeding amongst the leaves of all the trees. Vigour and thirst, emotion faced with a form that can neither be seen nor explained — that is poetry.

Let's not look for analogies in the various forms in which art is materialised; each must have its own liberty and its own frontiers. There are equivalents in art, each branch of the star develops independently, expands, and absorbs the world of its choice. But the parallelism that records the march of a new life will brand the era, without any theory.

To give each element its identity, its autonomy, the necessary condition for the creation of new constellations, since each has its own place in the group. The drive of the Word: upright, an image, a unique event, passionate, of dense colour, of intensity, in communion with life.
Art is a series of perpetual differences. For there is no measurable distance between "how are you?", the level on which people make their world grow, and human actions when seen from this angle of underwater purity. The strength to transmute this succession of ever-changing notions into *the instant* — that is the work of art. An Everlasting Sphere, a shape begotten by necessity, without a begetter.

The mind is alive with a new range of possibilities: to centralise them, to collect them under a lens that is neither material nor delimited — what is popularly called: the soul. The ways of expressing them, of transmuting them: the means. Bright as a flash of gold — the increasing beating of expanding wings.

Without pretensions to a romantic absolute, I present a few mundane negations.

A poem is no longer a formal act: subject, rhythm, rhyme, sonority. When projected on to everyday life, these can become means, whose use is neither regulated nor recorded, to which I attach the same weight as I do to the crocodile, to burning metals, or to grass. Eye, water, equilibrium, sun, kilometre, and everything that I can imagine as belonging together and which represents a potential human asset, is *sensitivity*. The elements love to be closely associated, truly hugging each other, like the cerebral hemispheres and the cabins of transatlantic liners.

Rhythm is the gait of the intonations we hear, but there is a rhythm that we neither see nor hear: the radius of an internal grouping that leads towards a constellation of order. Up to now, rhythm has been the beating of a dried-up heart, a little tinkle in putrid, padded wood. I don't want to put fences round what people call principles, when what is at stake is freedom. But the poet will have to be demanding towards his own work in order to discover its real necessity: order, essential and pure, will flower from this asceticism — (Goodness without a sentimental echo, its material side.)

To be demanding and cruel, pure and honest towards the work one is preparing and which one will be situating amongst men, new organisms, creations that live in the very bones of light and in the imaginative forms that action will take — (REALITY.)

The rest, called *literature*, is a dossier of human imbecility for the guidance of future professors.

The poem pushes up or hollows out the crater, remains silent, kills or shouts in an accelerating crescendo of speed. It will no longer depend on its visual image, on sense perception or on intelligence, but on its impact, or capability of transmuting the traces of emotions.
Comparison is a literary means which no longer satisfies us. There are different ways of formulating an image or of integrating it, but the elements will be taken from different and remote spheres.

Logic no longer guides us, and though it is convenient to have dealings with, it has become impotent, a deceptive glimmer, sowing the currency of sterile relativism, and we consider it from henceforth a light that has failed forever. Other creative powers, flamboyant, indefinable and gigantic, are shouting their liberty on the mountains of crystal and of prayer.

77

Liberty, liberty: not being a vegetarian, I'm not giving any recipes.

Obscurity must be creative if it is so pure a white light that it blinds our fellow-men. Where their light stops, ours starts. Their light is for us, in the fog, the microscopic and infinitely compact dance of the elements of darkness in imprecise fermentation. Is not matter in its pure state dense and unerring?

Under the bark of felled trees, I seek the image of things to come, of vigour, and in underground tunnels the obscurity of iron and coal may already be heavy with life.

pierre reverdy
"les ardoises du toit"
"les jockeys camouflés"

We know to what extent psychological art anaesthetises any movement — even if it is sometimes a literary movement — and the balance that *le Voleur de Talan* established in favour of the cosmic spirit. *Les ardoises du Toit* marks another state of equilibrium, a sensitivity specialising in soft, warm atmospheres, through elegance, the unexpected ending, first-rate and appreciable qualities, but it is definitely with *Les jockeys camouflés* that Reverdy achieves the maximum personal state of freedom: suddenly stopping and re-winding the movement starting from the other end, piling image upon image, dissipating the patchy fog, working on the reader's underwater matter, shocks of varying strength, dimension, level and price, poetry is certainly not a neurasthenic serum. Reverdy inclines more and more closely towards precise, free and cosmic CERTAINTY.
There are no laws, we can do whatever we like
let us use all means, every element calls to us,
post coitum exact flower of the sun.

francis picabia
"l'athlète des pompes funèbres"
"rateliers platoniques"

When it wants to destroy, the creative blood attains geyser-force, and collective, non-zoological vitality is heralded, inscribed in shorthand on the piano of anti-artistic isthmuses. In painting, Picabia has destroyed "beauty" and built his work with the left-overs: cardboard, money, the bird of the eternal mechanism, brain in an intimate relationship with the qualities of machines. Functions. Not merely the fabrication or expression of time, but the natural simplicity of an *immediate* notation with personal means. Whence the purity of his works. Romanticism is the descriptive exasperation of the gutter, of the plant, of the motor car, or a tender way of looking; disgust with observed systems leads Picabia on to the clear realities of machines; the rest is tranquillity, — immediate externalisation is the least effort or a naivety of means.

A stone expresses itself by the form and sometimes the luminosity of its facets, the vibration of the air passed through. I hate nature. Picabia doesn't like professionalism. His poems have no ending, his prose works never start. He writes without *working*, presents his personality, and doesn't control his feelings. Probes into the flesh of organisms. Neither word-stability nor music predominates, and I glide over his phrases towards a subterranean harmony. Picabia throws light on the rotation of realities and of mystery and reduces importances or pretensions to the relative equality of cosmic formation; he kills hysterical declamation and pathos on the little paths that we still find everywhere.

francis picabia
"pensées sans langage"

The philosophical myriapoda have broken some wooden or metal legs, and even some wings, between the stations Truth-Reality. There was always something that could not be grasped: LIFE.

To try to replace life by a private pleasure is an adventure that is sometimes amusing. (The remorseless adventures that insinuate themselves into art by its means, in order to destroy it slowly, revive the embers in the kernel, mutual interests, insinuations and obstacles system DADA movement.)

But to make a joke into something eternal and then starve it to death is ridiculous, it's the naive hello of the onanist, salvation army music, a motley pretension, a branch of the bourgeoisie flirting with art.

Anaemia isn't propagated on the continent, but you know about strength, microbes, flowers, alcohol, blood, inventions which diffuse their rain — aimlessly — or break like echoes on the solid, morning rock.

I'm thinking about the same need to impress — teach me how to say things seriously without sounding false — and it's always everyone else who is right.

The need to try to find explanations for what has no other reason than that it has quite simply been *done*, with no argument, with the minimum of criterion or criticism, is like self-kleptomania: like permanently sticking your own objects in different pockets. We also usually manage to build up a collection of some sort of moral speciality, to make it easy to pass judgment. Men are poor because they steal from themselves. It isn't a question of the difficulty of understanding modern life, but they steal elements of their own personalities.

PICABIA. His words fertilise metal. Whether meteor or wheel, urubu or hemstitched hurricane, he lets his feelings sleep in a garage. I place a hoot-owl in a hexagon, sing in hexameters, wear down and use up angles, howl "down with", and abuse. Geometry is dry, and old. I've seen a line leap in a different way. A line that has leapt kills theories; all we have to do then is look for adventure in the life of lines. A personal work, a work that shuns the absolute. And lives. Escapes. Full of silent sap. The mechanism of the aorta makes more noise than a life, its cog-wheels are on fire, awakening: typography of one's primary feelings, too simple to be deciphered so soon by the captains of science. My dear Picabia: "To live" without pretension, to dance on iron spikes, telegraphically, or to keep quiet on the equinoctial line, to know that at every instant — perpetua mobilia — it is today.

"Charm" and "pretty" apply to a moonlit night, to feelings, to paintings that sing and to songs that see, stick to traditions, insinuate themselves amongst the conventional and amongst painters.

Cubist and futurist painters, who ought to be allowing free vibration to their joy at having liberated appearances from a cumbersome and futile exterior, are becoming scientific and

84

academic. Theoretical propagation of carrion, blood pump. There are words which are also legions of honour. Hunting down the vulgar words that ensure the happiness of humanity, and the prestidigitatic prestige of prodigious predilections for the pleasure of the people who pay. Item: respect for bread and butter.

Ideas poison painting; if the poison bears the sonorous name of a big philological pot-belly, art becomes contagion and, if people rejoice at this intestinal musicality, the mixture becomes a danger for clean and sober men. It is only negative action that is necessary. Picabia has reduced painting to a simple structure; everyone will find therein the lines of his own life,
which go with time by railway and by wireless telephony
if he knows how to look without wondering why a cup is like a feeling.

open letter to jacques rivière

People these days no longer write with their race, but with their blood (what a platitude!) What, for the other sort of literature, was a *characteristic*, is today *temperament*. It more or less amounts to the same thing if we write a poem in Siamese or if we dance on a locomotive. It's only natural that the elderly don't notice that a new type of man is being created here, there and everywhere. With some insignificant variations in race the intensity is, I believe, the same everywhere, and if there is a common characteristic to be found in people who are creating today's literature, it will be that of anti-psychology.

. . . .

If one writes, it isn't a refuge: from every "point of view". I am not a professional writer and I have no literary ambitions. I should have become a successful adventurer, making subtle gestures, if I had had the physical force and nervous stamina to achieve this one exploit: not to be bored. One writes, too, because there aren't enough new men, out of habit, one publishes to try to find *men*, and to have an occupation (this in itself is very stupid.) There could be a solution: to resign oneself; quite simply: to do nothing. But you need enormous energy. And one has an almost hygienic need of complications.

art and hunting

Man-hunting has its roots and sources in one's topographical map in the discount bank; this goes without saying for that soft and subtle hallucination: man. This is normal and quite good, and quite foolish in the repetition that always attaches new importance to its latest apparition. But the results of man-hunting that are sold on the Stock Exchange need to be exhibited. With éclat and in a frame. It is here that a thick beard starts growing round the clear idea that I have, it hasn't yet had forty years of existence and of honest toil. I hate madness and its platonic form which is poetry and the absurd. "I hate" no longer has the unpleasant flavour that it used to have; it now means that I am smoking a cigarette.

Men are impenetrable; people who believe that men can interpenetrate each other like two hands crossed over a stomach, are wrong, are lying, and are getting a bad bargain. Values are as elastic as Lassalle's iron law of wages. Conflicts no longer exist because we are in summer's pocket. Bad speculation on the Institute, which used to express an insult, has brought us to see things on the same level: Place Vendôme, which couldn't contain pejorative mustard, is only a purely verbal statement.

Our ideas are clear and have no need of expression; the sport that consists of discharging, parallel with ideas, breaths which run and which discuss, is known to our best dialecticians. It is these breaths that try to dominate and to be in the right. But even the most beautiful women in France have only succeeded in showing themselves off at the Casino de Paris. Language is pretty threadbare, and yet it alone fills *the lives* of most men. All they know is the stories life has been able to tell them. Cracking jokes and the little pejorative air are for them the savour of language, the salt of life. Dada brutally intervened in this little cerebral domestic scene. But the most important inventions of the century have gone unnoticed: the tooth brush, God, aluminium. Therefore, Madam, mind you understand that a really dada product is something other than a brilliant label.

Dada has abolished nuances. Nuances don't exist in words, but in the brains of a few atrophied people where the cells are too congested. Simple notions which serve deaf-mutes as signs are entirely sufficient to express the four or five mysteries we have discovered.

Active influences are felt in politics, in commerce, in language. The whole world and everything in it has slid a bit to the left with us. Dada has stuck a nozzle into the hot bread. Little by little, big by big, it destroys. And we shall also see certain liberties that we take every day with feelings, and with social and moral life, becoming common practice. Already liberties are no longer being considered as crimes, but as itches.

dada proverb

Paul Eluard wants to achieve a concentration of words, crystallised as if for the people, but whose meaning remains null and void.

For example, the definition: "A proverb is a proverb", or: "A very proverby proverb." The dada proverb is the result of a multi-faceted sonority which comes out of all mouths with the force of inertia and with conviction of tone, but which alights with the tranquillity of time on wine. The motivating force behind the popular proverb is observation and experience, that of the dadaist proverb is a spontaneous concentration which penetrates in the guise of the former and may achieve the same degree and result: the little collective madness of a sonorous pleasure.

the bankruptcy of humour
reply to a questionnaire

I think we should invent new words to express better what we would like to mean by humour. I tried to introduce a meaningless word: "Dada."

Spontaneity closes the circuit of problems and the world which everyone creates in himself, purifies the work of art and generates the intimate communion of the soul with things. It is the great principle of subjectivism, the noble force of reality, the knowledge of the individual, that will characterise future art. The difference between Latin art (active simplicity) and German art, the result of heavy, systematic research until there is no longer any distinction between labour and creative spark, is defined by spontaneity. The work has wings, it takes its place amongst the elements of existence.

Isn't it enough to say: Rimbaud + Lautréamont + Jarry: the surest and most complex expression of French art? I don't think anyone will ever manage to put the most *cosmic-diverse* writers into pigeon-holes. Their richness, which belongs to the great apparitions and events of nature, their cosmic diversity, their supreme power of expressing the inexplicable simultaneously, without previous logical discussion, by severe and intuitive necessity, place them above all classifications and formulae.

I don't believe in influences, I sometimes think (at around 6 o'clock in the evening) of a spirit common to the period, but I declare myself an enemy of explanatory criticism and of objectivity. (Where is the fine, definitive and perfect system that we have been promised for the last 3,333 years, and the happiness of onanists? Philosophical discussions don't amuse me, for I am a partisan of the wireless.) I don't believe, either, in the mechanical elements of art, which are neither the regulation of the beautiful, nor its control, nor its consequence; but which we would be more likely to find at the peak of the intersection of two parallel lines, or in a submarine formation of stars and transchromatic aeroplanes. In the blood of stones, perhaps, in the obscurity of cellular metals and of cryptograms, and in the surge of images under the bark of trees.

I have seen "the deflatable man"
at the olympia

In the dead-tired courtyard, two men are sleeping — patches of difficult hours on the clock-face of human literatures. A cart, planks, furniture smelling of young wood and resin. Why are we sitting in the stalls watching him descend from sleep into death? We always leave by the stage door. Death is the colour of lead, his moustaches droop like the wings of worldly birds. His arms hang loosely. His chest is heavy. His leg muscles are like jelly. Everything is inflated with condemned breath. And that mass of accustomed material and flesh screws itself into a spiral in the centre of gravity that attracts it. His comrade is strong. He doesn't understand. He tries to sit him down on a chair. So as not to be next to a corpse any longer. He doesn't understand a thing. The other is still subsiding. He persists. Gets furious. Can't see anything but the tranquillity of balance. This lasts as long as the normal course of an illness. They are sitting side by side on chairs, and sleeping. The sun. They wake up. The deflatable man first. And scratches his head, which is seething with animal irritants.

note on the comte de lautréamont, or the cry

We know now that Lautréamont will be the Rimbaud of the poetry of today. "The Dictatorship of the Mind", presented without bothering about improvements or circumspection, is an affirmation of intensity, and steers every thought towards that noble, precise, sumptuous force, the only one worthy of interest — destruction.

Mal d'or or gold of dolour
Mal d'or or gold has destroyed the door of death.
His madness was not sublime — which is why it still lives on. Who dares to combat a reality because it is served up as a form of reproach?
TO SEE: necessity of a cerebral trigger.
Those people whose uncertainties show themselves in pretensions and whose pride rises in the form of cerebral saliva, those people for whom swamps and excrement have determined the rules of philosophical pity, will see, one of these days, this immeasurable malediction destroy their filthy, feeble muscles. The Comte de Lautréamont has gone beyond the tangential point which separates creation and madness. For him, creation is already mediocrity. On the other hand it is unpronounceable solemnity. The frontiers of wisdom are unexplored. Ecstasy devours them with neither hierarchy nor cruelty.
The dolour that freezes the brains, pulverises the crystal of its

blood, and leads the chaos of the sheathing of the hulls of old boats, of the lining of old coats, down a strange channel of pathetic regrets. Whether imaginary or exaggerated, dolour drinks silence, and accompanies the high-pitched force that is constantly trying to dissolve itself in the magic, universal delirium tremens.

The liberty of his faculties, which are bound by nothing, which he turns in all directions and especially towards himself, the strength to humble himself, to demolish, to cling to every blemish, with a sincerity far too intimate to interest us, are the highest human attitude because, transformed, as actions, they ought to culminate in the annihilation of that strange mixture of bones, flour and vegetation: humanity. The mind of this negative man, who was ever ready to be killed by the merry-go-round of the wind and to be trampled on by a hail of meteors, goes beyond the sickly hysteria of Jesus and other tireless windmills installed in the sumptuous apartments of history.

Don't love if you want to die in peace.

Mal d'or or gold of dolour

Mal d'or or gold has destroyed the door of death
by his brilliance and the music of the zephyr's frogs.

inside-out photography
man ray

It is no longer the object which, with the trajectories from its extreme points intersecting in the iris, projects a badly reversed image on the surface. The photographer has invented a new method; he presents to space an image that goes beyond it; and the air, with its clenched hands, and its head advantages, captures it and keeps it in its breast.

An eclipse revolves round a partridge: is it a cigarette case? The photographer makes the spit of thoughts revolve to the creaking of a badly-greased moon.

The light varies according to the giddiness of the pupil on the cold paper according to its weight and to the shock it produces. A wisp of a delicate tree enables us to anticipate metalliferous strata, mighty chandeliers. It illuminates the vestibule of the heart with a torch of snowflakes. And what interests us has neither reason nor cause, like a cloud that spits out its abundant voice.

But let us talk art. Yes, art. I know a man who does excellent portraits. The man is a camera. But, you say, the colour and the quivering of the brush are missing. That vague shiver that was first a weakness and later, in order to justify itself, called itself sensitivity. Human imperfection, it would appear, possesses more serious virtues than the exactitude of machines. And what about still lifes? We'd be glad to know whether hors-d'oeuvres, desserts and game hampers don't excite our appetite more. I listen to the humming of a tube in an oil field, a torpedo twists its mouth, the crockery breaks with the sound of domestic quarrels. Why not make the portrait of all that? Because this applies to a particular disturbance through a channel that leads to those sorts of emotion but which consumes neither eyes nor colours.

Painters have seen this, they've got together, talked for a long time, and discovered the laws of decomposition. And the laws of construction. And of circumvolution. And the laws of intelligence and of comprehension, of sales, of reproductions, of dignity and of museum-keeping. Other people arrived later with enlightened cries to say that what the first ones had produced was nothing but bird-droppings. They offered their merchandise instead, an impressionist blueprint reduced to a vulgar but attractive symbol. For a moment I believed in their idiots' cries, washed by the melting snow, but I soon discovered that it was only sterile jealousy that was tormenting them. They all ended up producing English postcards. After having known Nietzsche and sworn by their mistresses, after having pulled all the enamel paint off the corpses of their friends, they declared that beautiful children were just as admirable as good oil painting, and that the painting that sold for the most money was the best. Noble painting, with curly hair, in gilt frames. That's their marble; that's our piss.

When everything that people call art had got the rheumatics all over, the photographer lit the thousands of candles in his lamp, and the sensitive paper gradually absorbed the darkness between the shapes of certain everyday objects. He had invented the force of a fresh and tender flash of lightning which was more important than all the constellations destined for our visual pleasures. Precise, unique and correct mechanical deformation is fixed, smooth and filtered like a head of hair through a comb of light.

Is it a spiral of water, or the tragic gleam of a revolver, an egg, a glittering arc or a sluice gate of reason, a subtle ear with a mineral whistle or a turbine of algebraical formulae? As the mirror effortlessly throws back the image, and the echo the voice, without asking us why, the beauty of matter belongs to no one, for henceforth it is a physico-chemical product.

After the great inventions and storms, all the little swindles of the sensibility, of knowledge, and of the intelligence have been swept up into the pockets of the magical wind. The negotiator of luminous values takes up the bet laid by the stable-boys. The ration of oats they give morning and evening to the horses of modern art won't be able to disturb the passionate progress of his chess and sun game.

reply to a questionnaire

I got your letter at Hohenschwangau, the well-known site of the grotesque and shapeless memories of a mad king and another Wagner, where every step I take makes me realise the extent to which these false world-wide reputations still have a pernicious influence in France. From symbolism to instrumentalism, from orphism to paroxysm, from futurism to all the etceterisms that mix music and poetry, the singularly primitive idea of a "universal art" has tormented our writers' minds, and left traces of the Wagnerian bouillabaisse, that mysterious but undiscoverable sensitivity of which M. Maurice Barrès speaks in *Ennemi des Lois*.

1. Who is M. Thiers? Is he the author of the *Fêtes Galantes*? In that case there's no doubt about it: he's the worst writer in the French language. With a bit of subtlety on the part of the reader, we can substitute any other name for that of M. Thiers, even that of M. France. With the aid of progress, of perfected perfidy, of logic and of Wilde-like repartee, anyone can be right about anything. So far as I am concerned, the worst writer I had to read at school was M. France. He knows how to cheat his readers by well-worn seductive methods, and how to make his ambition pass for humanitarian good nature.

2. I won't talk about Massenet, that victorhugo of verlainian poetry. Nor of the Dumas-fils toothpaste, the false crocodile Rollinat, nor of the Sully vase and the broken Prudhomme, the boring Emile Augier ... I ought to quote all M. Doumic's history (I apologise for talking about the latter, because I believe he's still alive). Mallarmé has achieved a false reputation since the commercial zeal of the N.R.F. has acquainted us with those miserable *Vers de circonstance*, which reveal nothing but the vapidity and narrowness of mind of their author. I consider myself robbed by Mallarmé, because when re-reading his poems that I used to like, all I can see in them is a mechanical procedure of purely exterior syntax whose relative beauty lies in their workmanship. This is why the sympathy certain "constructivist" cubists feel towards him doesn't surprise me.

3. A writer whose reputation has been systematically usurped by the sweet, latent irony of a few snobs, is A. Dumas père. Yet his novels are extremely amusing, unique in the genre of direct literature, and more likeable since we have been sure that someone else wrote them.

I suggest that lovers of French poetry should count the numbers of copies sold of all the existing editions of Rimbaud. They will certainly be amazed.

The work of the Comte de Lautréamont, which I don't want to popularise here, had to suffer the malicious praise of Remy de Gourmont and Léon Bloy who, with their superior airs, classified it as a literary curiosity and declared that its author was mad. Those who know *Les Chants de Maldoror*, however, are aware that nothing counts in comparison with that marvellous anti-human epic. In every register, that of the illuminated assassin, of the irritating petit bourgeois, of the prophet conscious of his ridiculous position, with the grandeur that accepts and uses both the good and the bad, Lautréamont has formulated the greatest accusation against the human species. You know very well that this species is only distinguished from the others by its mania for writing and reading books.

In talking to you of these three writers whose reputations have been usurped, I can't help adding that I prefer the worst writers to the best, and false reputations to real ones.

lecture on dada

You already know that for the general public, and for you society people, a dadaist is the equivalent of a leper. But that's only a manner of speaking. When people talk to us at close quarters, they still treat us with the remains of elegance that they owe to their habit of believing in progress. But from ten metres away, their hate starts up again. That's dada. If you ask me why, I wouldn't be able to answer you.

Another characteristic of Dada is that we are always parting from our friends. We part, and we resign. The first person to resign from the Dada Movement *was I*. Everyone knows that Dada is nothing. I parted from Dada and from myself the moment I realised the true implication of *nothing*.

If I continue to do something, it's because it amuses me, or rather because I have a need for activity which I exert in all directions. In actual fact, the real dadas were always apart from Dada. Those people to whom dada was still important enough for them to part from it with éclat, were only acting with a view to their own personal advertisement, and proved that counterfeiters have always insinuated themselves with filthy worms amongst the purest and most lucid adventures of the spirit.

I know you're expecting some explanations about Dada. I'm not going to give you any. Explain to me why you exist. You've no idea. You'll say: I exist to make my children happy. But you know it's not really true. You'll say: I exist to protect my country from barbaric invasions. That's not enough. You'll say: I exist because God wants me to. That's a tale to tell the children. You'll never know why you exist, but you'll always allow yourselves to be easily persuaded to take life seriously. You'll never understand that life is a play on words, because you'll never be alone enough to refuse hate, judgments, and everything that needs a great effort, in favour of an even, calm state of mind in which everything is equal and unimportant.

Dada isn't at all modern, it's rather a return to a quasi-buddhist religion of indifference. Dada places an artificial sweetness on things, a snow of butterflies which have come out of a conjuror's head. Dada is immobility and doesn't understand the passions. You'll say that this is a paradox because Dada manifests itself by violent actions. Yes, the reactions of individuals contaminated by *destruction* are fairly violent, but once these reactions have been exhausted and annihilated by the continuous and progressive satanic insistence of a *"what's the use?"*, what remains and predominates is *indifference*. I could, what's more, with the same air of conviction, maintain the contrary.

I admit that my friends don't approve of this point of view. But this *Nothing* can only be expressed as a reflection of an individuality. That is why it will be useful to everybody, as no one accords any importance to anything but himself. I'm speaking of myself. That's already too much. How could I dare to speak of everyone at the same time and please everybody?

Nothing is more pleasant than to baffle people. The people one doesn't like. What's the use of explaining to them things that can only interest their curiosity? For people only like their own person, their income and their dog. This state of affairs derives from a false conception of property. If one is poor in spirit one possesses a sure and unshakeable intelligence, a ferocious logic and an immutable point of view. Try to become empty and to fill your brain cells haphazard. Go on destroying what you have in you. Indiscriminately. You could understand a lot of things, then. You aren't any more intelligent than we are, and we aren't any more intelligent than you.

Intelligence is an organisation like any other, social organisation, the organisation of a bank, or the organisation of a gossip-session. A society tea-party. Its purpose is to create order and introduce clarity where there is none. Its purpose is to create a hierarchy within a state. To make classifications for a rational piece of work. To separate questions of a material order from those of a moral order, but to take the former extremely seriously. Intelligence is the triumph of good breeding and pragmatism. Life, fortunately, is something different, and its pleasures are numberless. Their price cannot be evaluated in the currency of liquid intelligence.

These observations about everyday conditions have led us to a knowledge that constitutes our minimum of understanding, apart from the sympathy that links us, which is mysterious. We couldn't base it on principles. For everything is relative. What are Beauty, Truth, Art, Good, Liberty? Words which have a different meaning for every individual. Words which claim to make everybody agree, which is why they're usually written with capital letters. Words which do not have the moral value and the objective force that people are used to giving them. Their meaning changes from one individual to another, from one country to another. Men are different, it's their diversity that gives them their interest. There is no common basis in humanity's brains. The unconscious is inexhaustible and uncontrollable. Its strength is beyond us. It is as mysterious as the last particle of the brain cell. Even if we are familiar with it, who would dare state that we could reconstruct it as a viable generator of thoughts?

What use have philosophical theories been to us? Have they helped us to take a single step forward or backward? Where is "forward"; where is "backward"? Have they transformed our forms of contentment? We are. We quarrel, we fuss, we struggle. The intervals are sometimes pleasant, often mixed with a boundless tedium, a swamp adorned with the beards of moribund shrubs. We have had enough of the considered actions that have swollen beyond measure our credulity in the blessings of science. What we want now is *spontaneity*. Not because it is more beautiful or better

109

than anything else. But because everything that comes from us freely without any intervention from speculative ideas, represents us. We must accelerate this quantity of life that spends itself so readily here, there and everywhere. Art is not the most precious manifestation of life. Art does not have the celestial, general value that people are pleased to accord it. Life is far more interesting. Dada boasts of knowing the exact proportion that is to be given to art; it introduces it with subtle, perfidious means into the acts of everyday fantasy. And vice versa. In art, Dada brings everything back to an initial, but relative, simplicity. It mingles its caprices with the chaotic wind of creation and with the barbaric dances of savage tribes. It wants logic to be reduced to a personal minimum and literature to be primarily intended for the person who creates it. Words have a weight, too, and are used for an abstract construction. The absurd doesn't frighten me because, from a more elevated point of view, I consider everything in life to be absurd. It is only the elasticity of our conventions that makes a link between disparate acts. Beauty and Truth in art don't exist; what interests me is the intensity of a personality, transposed directly and clearly into its work, man and his vitality, the angle under which he looks at the elements and the way he is able to pick these ornamental words, feelings and emotions, out of the basket of death.

Dada tries to find out what words mean before using them, not from the point of view of grammar, but from that of representation. Objects and colours also pass through the same filter. It isn't a new technique that interests us, but the spirit. Why do you think we should bother about a pictorial, moral, poetic, social or poetic renovation? We all know that these stylistic renovations are only the successive uniforms of different historical eras, uninteresting questions and fashions and façades. We know very well that the people in Renaissance clothes were more or less the same as the people of today, and that Dchouang-Dsi was as dada as we are. You are making a mistake if you take Dada for a modern school, or even for a reaction against present-day schools. Several of my assertions have seemed to you to be old-fashioned and natural; this is the best proof that you were dadaists without knowing it, and perhaps even before the birth of dada.

You will often hear it said: Dada is a state of mind. You can be gay, sad, distressed, joyful, melancholy or dada. Without being literary, you can be romantics, you can be dreamers, weary, whimsical, shopkeepers, thin, convicts, conceited, pleasant or dada. Later, in the course of history, when Dada has become a precise, everyday word, and when its popular repetition has given it the meaning of an organic word with its necessary content, people will be dada with neither shame nor pejoration, for who today still thinks of literature in terms of calling a lake, a landscape, or a character, romantic? Slowly but surely a dada character is being formed.

Dada is more or less everywhere, just as it is; with its defects, with the differences between people which it accepts and regards with indifference.

We are very often told that we are incoherent, but people intend this word to convey an insult which I find rather hard to grasp. Everything is incoherent. The man who decides to have a bath but who goes to the cinema. The other man who wants to keep quiet but who says things that don't even come into his head. Another one who has an exact idea about something but who only manages to express the opposite in words which for him are a bad translation. No logic. Relative necessities discovered *a posteriori*, valid not from the point of view of their exactitude, but as explanations.

The acts of life have neither beginning nor end. Everything happens in a very *idiotic* fashion. That's why everything is the same. Simplicity is called dada.

To try to reconcile an inexplicable and momentary state with logic seems to me an amusing game. The convention of spoken language is amply sufficient, but for ourselves alone, for our inner games and our literature we don't need it any more.

In painting, things happen in the same way. Painters, technicians who do very well what a camera records much better, will carry on with the game. We'll play ours. We don't know why, nor how. With everything that comes to hand. It will be *badly done*, but we don't care.

111

The beginnings of Dada were not the beginnings of an art, but those of a disgust. Disgust with the magnificence of philosophers who for 3000 years have been explaining everything to us (what was the use?), disgust with the pretensions of those artists who were god's representatives on earth, disgust with passion, with real, morbid malice applied in cases where it isn't worth while, disgust with a new form of tyranny and restriction, which only accentuates men's instinct for domination instead of allaying it, disgust with all the catalogued categories, with the false prophets behind whom financial interests must be sought, with pride or with illness, disgust with people who separate good from evil, beauty from ugliness (for why is it more estimable to be red rather than green, left or right, tall or short?), disgust, finally, with the jesuitical dialectic that can explain everything and insert into people's poor brains oblique and obtuse ideas with neither roots nor base, all this by means of blinding artifices and the insinuating promises of charlatans.

Dada, after having again attracted the attention of the whole world to *death*, to its constant presence amongst us, works by destroying more and more, not in extent but in itself. Moreover it takes no pride in these disgusts, they bring it neither advantage nor profit. It doesn't even fight any more because it knows that there is no point in doing so, that none of this is of any importance. What interests a dadaist is his own way of living. But here we are reaching the places reserved for the great secret.

Dada is a state of mind. That is why it is transformed according to races and events. Dada is applicable to everything, and yet it is nothing, it *is* the point where *yes* and *no* meet, not solemnly in the castles of human philosophies, but quite simply on street corners like dogs and grasshoppers.

Dada is as useless as everything else in life.

Dada has no pretensions, which is how life ought to be.

Perhaps you'll understand me better if I tell you that dada is a virgin microbe that insinuates itself with the insistence of air into all the spaces that reason hasn't been able to fill with words or conventions.

Notes

SEVEN DADA MANIFESTOS

Monsieur Antipyrine's Manifesto was read at the first Dada demonstration in Zurich (Salle Waag), on July 14th 1916. Published in "La Première Aventure céleste de M. Antipyrine", 1916.

Dada Manifesto 1918 was read in Zurich (Salle Meise), on March 23rd 1918. Published in "Dada 3", 1918.

Unpretentious Proclamation was read at the 8th Soirée Dada in Zurich (Salle Kaufleuten), on April 8th 1919. Published in "Anthologie Dada", 1919.

Manifesto of Monsieur Aa the Antiphilosopher was read at the Grand Palais des Champs-Elysées on February 5th 1920. Published in "Littérature" no. 13, 1920.

Tristan Tzara's Manifesto was read at the *Université populaire*, on February 19th 1920. Published in "Littérature" no. 13, 1920.

Monsieur Aa the Antiphilosopher sends us this Manifesto was read at the Dada Festival at the Salle Gaveau, Paris, on May 22nd 1920. Published in "391" no. 12, 1920.

Dada Manifesto on Feeble Love and Bitter Love was read at the Galerie Povolozky, Paris, on December 12th 1920. Published in "La Vie des Lettres" no.4, 1921.

The Appendix: *How I became charming, likeable and delightful* was read at the Galerie Povolozky, Paris, on December 19th 1920. Published in "La Vie des Lettres" no. 4, 1921.

115

LAMPISTERIES

Note on Art, published in "Dada 1", Zurich, July 1917.
Note on Negro Art, published in "Sic", Paris, September-October 1917.
Note on Art — H. Arp, published in "Dada 2", Zurich, December 1917.
Guillaume Apollinaire, published in "Dada 2", Zurich, December 1917.
Pierre Reverdy, published in "Dada 2", Zurich, December 1917.
Pierre Albert-Birot, published in "Dada 2", Zurich, December 1917.
Note on Negro Poetry, published in "Sic", Paris, November 1918.
Guillaume Apollinaire is dead,
R. Huelsenbeck, published in "Dada 4 et 5", Zurich, May 1919.
Note on Poetry, published in "Dada 4 et 5", Zurich, May 1919.
Pierre Reverdy, published in "Dada 4 et 5", Zurich, May 1919.
Francis Picabia, published in "Dada 4 et 5", Zurich May 1919.
Francis Picabia, published in "Littérature", December 1919, and as a preface to "Unique Eunuque", January 1920.
Open Letter to Jacques Rivière, published in "Littérature", December 1919.
Art and Hunting, published in "Salon Dada", catalogue of the Dada Exhibition at the Galerie Montaigne, Paris, June 1921.
Dada Proverb, published in "Invention no. 1 et Proverbe no. 6",

Paris, July 1921.

The Bankruptcy of Humour, Reply to a Questionnaire, published in "Aventure", Paris, November 1921.

I have seen "the deflatable man" at the Olympia, published in "Littérature", March 1922.

Note on the Comte de Lautréamont, or the Cry, published in "Littérature", March 1922.

Inside-out Photography, preface to the album, "Les champs délicieux" by Man Ray, Paris, December 1922.

Reply to a Questionnaire, written on September 12th 1922 at Hohenschwangau (Bavaria).

Lecture on Dada, given at Weimar and at Jena on September 23rd and 25th 1922, published in "Merz", Hanover, January 1924.